The
WORST-CASE SCENARIO
POCKET GUIDE
CATS

By David Borgenicht &
Ben H. Winters

Illustrations by Brenda Brown

D0342086

CHRONICLE BOOKS
SAN FRANCISCO

Copyright © 2009 by Quirk Productions, Inc.

All rights reserved. No part of this book may be
reproduced in any form without written permission
from the publisher.

Worst-Case Scenario® and The Worst-Case Scenario
Survival Handbook™ are trademarks of Quirk
Productions, Inc.

Library of Congress Cataloging in Publication Data
available.

ISBN: 978-0-8118-7047-4

Manufactured in China
Designed by Jenny Kraemer
Illustrations by Brenda Brown
Visit www.worstcasescenarios.com

10 9 8 7 6 5 4 3 2 1

Chronicle Books LLC
680 Second Street
San Francisco, CA 94107
www.chroniclebooks.com

CONTENTS

Introduction . . . 4

1 Cat House . . . 9
Living with a Cat

2 The Purr-fect Storm . . . 39
Health and Hairballs

3 Cat-itude . . . 69
Behavior

Index . . . 90

Acknowledgments . . . 93

About the Authors . . . 94

INTRODUCTION

When cats are kittens, they behave like actual pets. They are our playmates, our cuddle companions, our lap pillows.

But as they grow up, they become less and less like our pets. They can be mercurial in their affections—snuggling up to us when they need it, haughtily walking away from us when they feel more antisocial. They act as if they own us, or as if they are gracing us with their presence. And sometimes, they even become downright difficult, scratching new furniture, marking territory, coughing up hairballs, proudly displaying their caught prey, hissing or biting. In short, they become more and more like us. Although much of the time they are still our bundles of love, they can become worst-case scenarios with the twitch of a tail.

That's where this handy little volume comes in. *The Worst-Case Scenario Pocket Guide: Cats* offers step-by-step solutions to the most difficult feline situations, from breaking up a catfight to getting your cat out from under a bed, and from treating a catnip addict to getting your cat to accept your new baby. We've also included handy charts and instant solutions for a variety of catty conundrums. If you need to know what you can make from errant hairballs, look no further.

We're not trying to frighten you away from cat, um, ownership. We just want you to be ready if your precious Princess unexpectedly turns into a saber-toothed nightmare.

So be prepared—and take solace in the fact that this book can be used as an emergency litter scooper (and easily cleaned off).

—The Authors

As every cat owner knows,
nobody owns a cat.
—Ellen Perry Berkeley

CHAPTER 1
LIVING WITH A CAT

CAT HOUSE

HOW TO GET A CAT OUT FROM UNDER THE BED

⭐ Run the can opener.
Go to the kitchen and run an electric can opener.

⭐ Sweep the cat out from under the bed.
Use a broom or mop to nudge or sweep the cat from his hiding place.

⭐ Loudly show affection for another pet.
Sit in an area visible from your cat's position underneath the bed. Hold another cat, dog, or child in your lap and stroke the child or pet gently. Praise the other animal or child in the way you would praise your cat.

Loudly show affection for another pet.

11.   *Living with a Cat*

✪ Sit, roll, or bounce around on the bed.
Move abruptly and make loud noises on top of the bed to try to scare the cat out from under it.

✪ Stick your head under the bed.
Make loud hissing noises to scare the cat into running out from under the bed.

✪ Make a line of treats.
Create a trail of cat treats starting at the edge of the bed and continuing several feet past it leading out of the room. When the cat follows the treats from under the bed and out the door, shut the door behind him.

How to Get a Cat Out of a Tree

1 Clear psychological obstacles.
Remove whatever frightening person, dog, or possum caused your cat to go up the tree.

2   Lean a ladder against the tree.

3   Cook bacon.
Fry fresh bacon in a skillet on the stove.

4   Bring the freshly fried bacon outside.
Place it at the foot of the ladder and wait for your cat to descend.

5   Grab your cat.

Be Aware

- Throughout the rescue process, calmly call your cat's name to prevent him from becoming too anxious or upset.
- Many cats will resist coming out of a hiding place, even in the face of extreme hunger or weather conditions.
- Cats (especially kittens) stuck in high trees can fall prey to raccoons, possums, owls, and other predators.

INSTANT SOLUTION

BATHE A CAT

Talk soothingly to your cat, then quickly submerge her in lukewarm water. After shampooing, rinse the cat using a hose or large measuring cup. Have a towel ready.

HOW TO GET RID OF CAT PEE ODORS

To Clean Fresh Cat Pee Odors

1 Identify the affected areas.
Crouch down on all fours and crawl
around your home like a cat, focusing on
your cat's favorite locations. Sniff until
you find the sources of the odor. Look for
amber-colored puddles of urine.

2 Blot up the urine.
Press firmly down on the affected area
with a damp towel. Blot only. Rubbing
will widen the radius of the stain.

3 Cover the affected area with a layer of
paper towels.
Stand on the layer of paper towels until
the urine stains have soaked through (wear
shoes). Repeat with a fresh layer of paper

*Crouch down on all fours and crawl around your home
like a cat, focusing on your cat's favorite locations.*

towels until there is no longer any
moisture on the paper towels when
you pick them up.

4 Spray the affected area with a mixture of
vinegar and water.
Prepare a solution of one tablespoon of
vinegar to one liter of warm water. Use a
misting spray bottle to cover the affected
area with the solution. Let the solution
sit for one minute, and then re-blot with
paper towels.

5 Sprinkle the affected area with
baking soda.
Wait 24 hours and thoroughly vacuum up
the baking soda.

To Clean Old Cat Pee Odors

1 Turn on a black light.
Turn off all the lights and plug in a black-
light lamp. Shine the light across the room

and along areas frequented by your cat in search of old urine stains, which will glow under the black light. Move furniture and investigate all corners of the room. Check each room of the house.

2 Coat urine-stained carpeting in a mixture of lukewarm water and vinegar.
Use one part vinegar to three parts water, or if the smell is especially strong, two parts vinegar to three parts water. Wait 24 hours.

3 Prepare a shampoo solution.
If the smell persists, prepare a solution of a half gallon of water, a half pint of rubbing alcohol, a half-tablespoon of ammonia, one tablespoon of vinegar, and a half teaspoon of dish detergent. Vigorously shampoo the solution into the carpet.

4 Rinse solution from carpet.

5 Apply a solution of baking soda and hydrogen peroxide on urine-stained upholstery.

Mix half a box of baking soda into three cups of water. Add hydrogen peroxide until the solution has a thick, paint-like consistency. Spread liberally on the affected area; let soak for 12 hours before scrubbing off. Test the solution on a small, hidden portion of the upholstery before applying to the entire piece of furniture.

6 Scrub stained hardwood with white vinegar.

If the stain persists, sand the stain off the wood with sandpaper or a sander.

Be Aware

- Because cats do not drink as much water as other animals, their urine is extremely concentrated and therefore has an extremely unpleasant scent. The longer the urine is allowed to sit, the worse the odor gets, as various bacteria feed on the waste products contained in it.

- The smell of cat urine stimulates cats to urinate, so even a small trace of lingering odor will cause the problem to recur in the same spot.
- A cat that frequently urinates outside his litter box may have a medical problem such as a urinary tract infection. He may also be marking his territory in response to the addition of a new person or cat to the household.
- Test any solution on a small portion of carpet, upholstery, or hardwood before applying to a large surface.
- If the combination of vinegar and water, followed by baking soda, is ineffective, purchase and apply a commercial product; only use products marked "enzyme cleaners," not "deodorizers."

THINGS TO DO SO
YOUR CAT IS NOT LONELY
WHEN YOU'RE AWAY

- Give him a new toy just before leaving.

- Leave the TV on, or attach a timer that switches it on periodically.

- Leave the radio on, tuned at low volume to a talk-radio station.

- Put a cardboard cutout of yourself in the room.

- Make a mobile with pictures of yourself and hang it over your cat's litter box.

- Leave behind an old shirt for him to smell and play with.

- Leave the curtains open so he can see outside.

- Ask a neighbor to stop by.

- Talk to him through the answering machine.

- Leave your desktop computer on and talk to him via video conference.

- Hang a mirror at the cat's eye-level.

HOW TO MAKE TWO CATS GET ALONG

1 Create a "safe space" for the new cat.
Set up a small room with the cat's litter box, food, water, and toys. If one new cat is being introduced to a household, the "safe space" should be for her, while the previous cat remains at large in the rest of the home. If two new cats are simultaneously introduced to the household and one another, create the safe space for the cat that appears more shy and nervous.

2 Prohibit the original cat from entering the safe space for one week.
The original cat is likely to prowl around the perimeter and sniff under the door, which is okay. If the original cat begins

Show affection to the new cat in front of the original cat.

23. *Living with a Cat*

hissing or growling at the door, move
him away.

3 Show affection to both cats.
Spend equal amounts of time with each
cat, petting, playing, and feeding treats to
both. Let the original cat see you go into
the "safe room," so he is aware that you are
showing affection to the new cat. Show
affection to the original cat just outside
the door of the safe space, so the new cat
is aware of it.

4 Switch the cats' bedding blankets so they
become familiar with each other's scent.
Encourage them to explore the smell.
Repeat at least once a day during the one
week "safe space" transition.

5 Open the door.
After a week of separation, introduce the
cats to each other by allowing them to
occupy the same space.

6 | Closely monitor the cats' interaction. Immediately break up any fighting and return the new cat to her safe space if she has not already retreated. Leave the cats separated again for one hour.

7 | Reward nonaggressive behaviors. When the cats are playing nicely, or ignoring one another, distribute extra treats, catnip, and petting sessions. Praise both cats equally.

8 | Separate the cats permanently. If they continue to hiss at each other every time they meet for two months, one or both may be temperamentally unable to socialize with the other.

Be Aware
Cats that have been spayed or neutered are less territorial and get along better with other cats.

HOW TO BREAK UP A CAT FIGHT

1 Identify the aggressor.
Look for the cat that is on top of the other one. This is the aggressor.

2 Scold the aggressor.
In a loud voice, yell "NO," "STOP," or "THAT'S ENOUGH!" and the aggressor's name.

3 Make loud noises.
Clap your hands, stomp your feet, or bang two pot lids together.

4 Physically separate the cats.
Use a long-handled implement such as a mop or broom, to nudge the cats apart. If the fight is happening outside, throw water or turn a hose onto them.

Use a long-handled broom to nudge the cats apart.
Throw water or turn a hose on them.

5 "Scruff" the aggressor cat.
Grasp the aggressor cat by the loose skin at the back of his neck. Remove him from the other cat and push him toward the floor with firm but gentle pressure. Hiss loudly. While the aggressor is being scruffed, allow the victim cat to flee the area.

6 Keep the cats apart.
Separate the aggressor and victim cat for one hour. If aggressive behavior resumes, establish a "safe room" for the aggressor and reintroduce the cats to each other over a week-long period.

Be Aware
- Do not get in the middle of a cat fight and try to pry the cats apart physically. The cats will instinctively treat you as another combatant.

- Play fighting is a part of a healthy cat's social life and needn't be discouraged. If the cats are frequently switching roles (one chasing, the other being chased; one pouncing, the other acting as "prey") and neither cat is hissing or showing teeth, do not intervene.

INSTANT SOLUTION

TREAT A CAT BITE

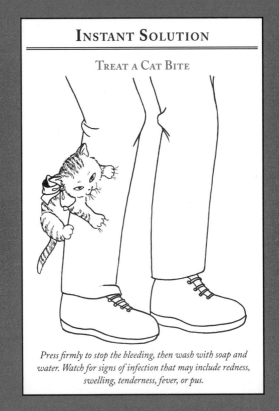

Press firmly to stop the bleeding, then wash with soap and water. Watch for signs of infection that may include redness, swelling, tenderness, fever, or pus.

HOW TO KITTEN-PROOF YOUR HOME

✪ Examine your entire house as if you were a kitten.

Get down on all fours and move from room to room, peering into every exposed area. Identify and remove all small objects that might be swallowed by a curious kitten, such as screws (which can be lodged in a cat's throat), as well as any yarn or string (which can create digestive problems if ingested).

✪ Rub electrical and computer cords with spicy substances.

Liberally coat all exposed power cords with chili powder or cayenne pepper to create a distasteful impression the first time the kitten attempts to chew on them.

Tire your cat out with toys.

✪ Tie up curtains.
Loop the curtains so that the kitten cannot jump high enough to scratch them.

✪ Remove dangerous objects from the kitchen counter.
Move scissors, knives, and sharp utensils into locked drawers.

✪ Vigorously exercise your cat.
A cat's curiosity is often a manifestation of excess energy. Tire your cat out with long walks, running up and down the stairs, or chasing a "kitty lure."

✪ Surround your plants with wrinkled aluminum foil.
Place a loose layer of aluminum foil on the soil around the base of the plant. Lay more foil around the base of the pot itself. Kittens hate the feel of walking on foil and will avoid the plants.

✪ Keep the toilet lid down.

✪ Use garbage cans that require foot pressure to be opened.

✪ Move bird cages and fish bowls to areas of the home that are inaccessible to your cat. On average, a cat can jump five times as high as it is long. If you have no place to keep other pets that will not be out of reach of the cat, remove them from the household.

✪ Keep toxic substances out of reach. Secure cleaning products, prescription drugs, and vitamins behind closed cabinets. Many household substances, such as aspirin and antifreeze, can be deadly to cats.

✪ Screen the fireplace. A kitten may mistake cooling ashes for a litter box.

✪ Secure toilet paper rolls.
Use a large binder clip to secure the
unused portion of toilet paper, so your
kitten cannot tug on the exposed piece.

Be Aware
- Your new kitten will not necessarily
  have an instinctive aversion to heat.
  Be on guard when cooking or using
  the fireplace.
- Kittens need stimulation for their natural
  curiosity. A cat fort or scratching post
  will divert them from roaming the home
  in search of places to play.

THINGS THAT ARE TOXIC TO CATS

Item
Milk
Poinsettias, lilies, many other houseplants
Dog food
Onions
Garlic
Chocolate
Cherry tomatoes
Raw salmon
Soy
Yeast
Aspirin
Acetaminophen
Antifreeze

Danger to Cat

Various stomach problems

Stomachaches, various forms of poisoning

Vomiting, diarrhea

Anemia

Anemia

Potential kidney failure

Various stomach problems

Salmon poisoning, death

Thyroid malfunction

Allergies, bloating, urinary tract problems

Gastrointestinal problems, respiratory problems, kidney failure

Severe blood ailments, death

Severe kidney damage, death

THE PURR-FECT STORM

HOW TO WEAN
A KITTEN

1 Pour the kitten's formula out of her
bottle into a shallow dish.
Place the dish on a towel or blanket.

2 Dip your forefinger in the formula.
Offer the formula on your finger to your
kitten. Encourage your kitten to lick the
formula off your hand. Taste the formula
and exclaim that it is "yummy." Do not
scold or punish your kitten if she is unin-
terested in drinking the formula this way,
or if she bites your fingertip. Repeat until
the kitten approaches the saucer directly
for formula.

3 Watch your kitten while she laps
the formula.
If your kitten falls into the dish, take
her out.

Retrieve your kitten if she falls into the dish.

4 | Add solid food to the formula.
At the next feeding, mix a teaspoon of wet cat food into the formula, creating a thin paste. Encourage your kitten to lap at the paste. Have a bottle of formula on hand, in case she will not eat from the saucer. Try again at the following feeding.

5 | Steadily increase the proportion of wet food in the dish.
Each day add more, until your kitten is eating only solid food.

6 | Try different brands of cat food.
If your kitten remains resistant to the solid food, experiment with other varieties. After she is eating wet cat food exclusively, and no longer takes formula, begin to offer dry food.

Be Aware

- Most bottle-fed kittens are ready to be weaned when they are around four weeks old.
- The change in diet from formula to solid food can affect your kitten's digestive system. Do not be alarmed during the transition period if your kitten experiences frequent bouts of diarrhea.

BREED/PERSONALITY MISMATCHES

If You Are . . .	Don't Get a . . .	
In need of peace and quiet	Siamese	
Seeking companionship	Maine Coon	
Highly allergic	Persian	
Lazy	Norwegian Forest Cat	
A neat freak	Abyssinian	
Living in cramped quarters	British Shorthair	

Because They Are . . .

Very vocal, especially when they feel ignored

Particularly aloof

Long-haired, and always shedding

Hyperactive

Extremely curious, into everything

Fat

HOW TO TREAT A CATNIP ADDICTION

1   Admit that your cat has a problem.
Look for signs of catnip-high, such as
half-lidded eyes, copious drooling, and
constant or excessive leaping or romping.
An addicted cat will ignore its owner, fel-
low cats, and scratching posts, focusing all
her attention on toys infused with catnip.
When no catnip is available, an addicted
cat may display catnip-seeking behavior,
such as nuzzling, sitting in her owner's lap,
purring, and other displays of affection.
Extended periods without catnip may lead
to symptoms such as listlessness, loss of
appetite, and irritability.

Watch for signs of catnip-seeking behavior such as nuzzling, purring, or other displays of affection.

47. *Health and Hairballs*

2 Gradually reduce your cat's access to catnip.
Remove all catnip toys but one. Only make this toy available for limited periods of the day. Gradually reduce the duration and frequency of these periods of exposure until she regains interest in her other toys and aspects of her life.

3 Protect against acting-out behaviors.
During the transition period, separate your cat from other cats, animals, and children in the home. While adjusting to lessened catnip exposure, your cat may lash out by scratching or urinating on other members of the household.

4 Go cold turkey.
Confine your cat in a bedroom or bathroom for 24 hours with plenty of food and water, and a fresh litter box. Your cat may try to bargain with you by purring, or yowling. In a stern but loving voice,

explain to your cat that what you are doing is for her own good.

5 Secure your cat's environment.
After successfully helping your cat kick her habit, ensure that she stays away from other cats that are still using. Rid your home of all catnip toys and destroy any catnip plants and residue. If your neighbors are cat owners who give catnip to their own cats, make them aware that your cat has a problem.

Be Aware
Other names for catnip include *cataria*, catmint, and field balm. Valerian is a different herb that evokes similar response patterns in some cats.

INSTANT SOLUTION

REMOVE BURRS FROM CAT FUR

Use a metal comb to tease out each burr.
If embedded deeply, cut out burrs with scissors.

HOW TO DEAL WITH AN OBESE FELINE

★ Reduce feedings.
Create four set feeding times per day.
Remove the food dish between feedings
so that your cat cannot continue to eat
whenever he wants. Do not feed your cat
scraps from the table.

★ Cut down portion sizes.
Ignore the recommended portion size on
the container of cat food. An active adult
cat should eat between six and ten ounces
of canned food per meal.

★ Keep your cat's water bowl full.
Inadequate hydration can lead to a variety
of kidney ailments in cats and kittens.

Health and Hairballs

Move your cat's food to the top or bottom of the stairs.

✪ Give your cat a balanced diet.
Feed your cat 75 percent canned wet foods
and 25 percent low-calorie dry foods.
Wet foods are higher in protein and lower
in carbohydrates than dry foods, better
approximating the in-the-wild cat diet of
mice, birds, and rabbits.

✪ Encourage your cat to eat natural prey.
Support your outdoor cat's pursuit
of birds and mice, which are high in
protein. Chasing such animals is also
good exercise.

✪ Reward your cat in ways other than
offering food treats.
Demonstrate affection and reward positive
behavior with vigorous petting, catnip
sessions, or a favorite toy.

✪ Place food at the top of the stairs.
When your cat falls asleep after eating,
move the food to the bottom of the stairs,

so she must take the stairs again for the next meal.

★ Dangle a catnip-stuffed toy just above your cat's head.
When she leaps up to paw it, jerk it away, causing your cat to jump repeatedly in attempts to play with the toy.

★ Attach a cat toy by a string from the back of your belt.
Run around the room in circles so your cat chases you.

Be Aware

- One pound of extra weight on a cat is equivalent to five to ten pounds of extra weight on a human.
- Dangers associated with obesity in cats include diabetes, heart failure, and kidney failure.
- Cats are natural meat eaters and cannot thrive on a vegetarian diet.

ALTERNATE USES FOR UNUSED KITTY LITTER

To eliminate unwanted odors:
• Leave two tablespoons in an open bowl in the back of the refrigerator.
• Sprinkle a handful in the bottom of a kitchen trashcan or diaper pail.
• Place a handful in an ashtray.

For traction:
• Sprinkle under tire wheels when stuck in snow or mud.
• Sprinkle ahead of each footstep as you walk down an icy road or sidewalk.

To remove the algae from koi ponds:
• Add a half pound of kitty litter for every 1000 gallons of pond water.

To absorb spills:
• Spread a half-inch layer on fresh liquid spills on your carpet or rug. After ten minutes, sweep up kitty litter before vacuuming rug.

HOW TO TOILET TRAIN YOUR CAT

1 Move the litter box next to the toilet.

2 Incrementally raise the litter box to the level of the toilet.
Place telephone books or encyclopedias under the litter box, one at a time, until the box is at the same height level as the toilet. Wait each time until your cat is adjusted and comfortable with the new level before raising the level again.

3 Leave the litter box in this raised, toilet-adjacent position.
The box should be positioned so that the cat must step across the toilet to access her litter box. Leave it there until your cat is accustomed to the feel of walking on the toilet seat.

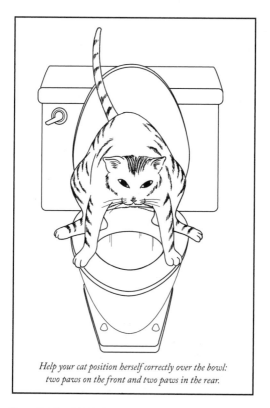

*Help your cat position herself correctly over the bowl:
two paws on the front and two paws in the rear.*

4 Move the litter box on top of the toilet seat.
Leave it in this position for several days, so your cat becomes used to doing her business on top of the toilet. When you use the toilet, remove the litter box and then replace it when you're done.

5 Remove the litter box from the top of the toilet seat.

6 Place a mixing bowl in the toilet.
Select a bowl that fits snugly in the toilet bowl. Fill it with two to three inches of cat litter. Humans using the toilet should first remove the metal mixing bowl.

7 Position the cat's feet.
Watch your cat constantly over a period of several days. Every time she goes to the toilet to urinate or defecate, help her set her feet correctly on the lid of the toilet: Two paws on the front and two paws in

the rear, so she is squatting over the mixing bowl.

8 Replace the cat litter in the mixing bowl with water.
Continue helping your cat position herself correctly over the bowl, and encourage her, so she becomes used to the sound of doing her business into water. Each time your cat relieves herself successfully in the mixing bowl, empty it into the toilet and flush it while she watches.

9 Remove the mixing bowl from the toilet.
Once your cat has become used to relieving herself into water while sitting on the toilet, take the mixing bowl away.

Be Aware
Once your cat is toilet-trained, the door to the bathroom and the toilet lid need to be left open, so the cat enjoys free access to the toilet.

THINGS YOU CAN TRAIN CATS TO DO	THINGS YOU CAN'T TRAIN CATS TO DO
• Come when called for dinner	• Sit
• Use litter box	• Stay
	• Fetch
	• Roll over
	• Speak
	• Shake
	• Come
	• Go
	• Get the newspaper
	• Pull a sled
	• Rescue you in the snow
	• Lead you if you are blind

HOW TO DEAL WITH CAT ALLERGIES

✪ Recognize allergic symptoms.
Symptoms of cat allergy include sneezing,
itching, runny nose, and nasal congestion.
Also look out for itchiness or hoarseness
in the throat, escalating to coughing
and wheezing.

✪ Eliminate other possible allergen sources
from your home.
Remove any mold, cockroaches, dust
mites, or dogs.

✪ Keep your cat out of your bedroom.
Do not allow your cat to sleep with you in
your bed at night.

Don protective gear when at home with the cat.

✪ Confine your cat to one area of the home.
Do not allow your cat in the kitchen, dining room, or other area where food is stored or consumed. Erect cat-proof barriers at the door to the designated cat area. If your cat escapes into the cat-free zone, chase her back into the designated area by stamping your feet.

✪ Wash your hands after touching your cat.
Use antibacterial soap. Dry your hands thoroughly. Also, wash your hands after touching anything your cat has touched.

✪ Avoid touching your eyes while in your home.
Introduction of allergens directly into the eyes can exacerbate and prolong allergic reactions.

✪ Wear a surgical mask and gloves.
Don protective gear when at home with the cat.

★ Replace surfaces prone to collecting cat allergens.

Redecorate with easy-to-clear items and elements. Remove all carpets and replace with hard-surface flooring. Replace uphol-stered furniture with firm solid surfaces or vinyl-covered pieces.

★ Clean your home frequently.

Run a vacuum steamer over all carpeted surfaces in the home at least twice a week. Scrub uncarpeted floors and other exposed surfaces with a commercial antibacterial cleaning solution.

Be Aware

- There is some evidence that short-haired cats are less allergenic than long-haired cats because they shed less. However, the enzymes excreted by cats that cause reactions exist in the cat's feces, dead skin flakes, urine, hair, and saliva. For this reason, hairless or short-haired cats are only marginally less allergy inducing.

- Some cat breeds are thought to be hypoallergenic, meaning they are less likely to create allergic reactions in people. These breeds include Devon, Cornish Rex, Sphynx, and Siberian.
- Allergens can never be completely removed from a residence that is shared with a cat.

LIKE CATS AND DOGS

Range in size

Average amount of fecal matter (per day)

Causes allergies

Catches mice

Watches for burglars

Needs to be walked

Wakes you up in the morning by slobbering on your face

Leaves you alone when you want to be left alone

Makes loud noise for no reason

Requires constant attention

Requires constant affection

Requires constant positive reinforcement

Eats its own fecal matter

Dogs	Cats
4 to 200 pounds	3 to 30 pounds
3/4 pound	5 to 6 tablespoons
Yes	Yes
Yes	Yes
Yes	No
Yes	No
Frequently	Rarely
No	Yes
Yes	No
Yes	No
Yes	No
Yes	No
Sometimes	Sometimes

CHAPTER 3
BEHAVIOR

CAT-ITUDE

HOW TO DEAL WITH A CAT WHO IS AFRAID OF MICE

1 Construct a toy mouse.

Cut an athletic sock about six inches above the toe; discard the top of the sock. Using a permanent marker, draw eyes, a nose, and whiskers on the toe of the sock. A mitten, similarly decorated, may also serve as a "mouse."

2 Stuff the toy mouse with catnip and tie it closed.

Tie the end of the sock or mitten closed with a six-inch length of yarn, leaving one end loose to form the tail. Tie another two-foot length of yarn around the middle of the mouse.

Dangle a toy mouse stuffed with catnip in front of your cat.

3 Go into a small room with your cat. Close the door.

4 Dangle the toy mouse in front of your cat.
In a soft and encouraging voice, say "Get it! Get the mouse!" while you dangle the mouse closer and closer to your cat's face. If your cat is not sufficiently drawn to the catnip to pounce on the toy, rub the outside of the mouse with additional catnip.

5 Drop the mouse.
As soon as your cat attacks the toy mouse, let the yarn go slack so the mouse falls to the ground and your cat can leap upon it. Gently tug the yarn so that the mouse simulates movement after your cat has attacked it to keep her engaged. Repeat until cat pounces on the mouse toy.

6 | Celebrate.
Say "Good Kitty! Brave Kitty!" Do not attempt to pet the cat while she is attacking the mouse; she may bite or claw you in her excitement.

Be Aware

- Do not starve your cat in an effort to make her more "hungry for mice." A hungry cat will not have the energy to hunt.
- As an alternative to catnip, stuff the mouse toy with the herb Valerian, two tablespoons of wet cat food, or several small bells so it makes a jingling noise while bouncing in the air.

THINGS TO MAKE
OUT OF HAIRBALLS

- Fake beard

- Fake mustache

- Fake sideburns

- Daisy chain

- Piano dampers

- Chair-leg attachments (to protect hardwood floors)

- Hairball "monkey"

- Christmas tree ornament

- Pillow stuffing

- Scarf

HOW TO GET A CAT TO CUDDLE

1 Play soothing classical music.

2 Do aerobic exercise.
Perform jumping jacks, sit-ups, or push-ups until you are lightly perspiring. Elevated skin temperature and a sheen of perspiration are attractive to warm-blooded mammals such as cats.

3 Remove your shirt.

4 Sit down in a large, reclining chair. Recline the chair by 45 degrees. Move your butt forward so your lap space is maximized.

Do aerobic exercise. Perspiration is attractive to cats.

5 Call your cat's name in an encouraging voice.
Cats will also respond to any other words.

6 Purr.
Bring your tongue up to the roof of your mouth and gently exhale, blowing air over your tongue and through your front teeth. Alternate between purring and calling your cat's name.

7 Lightly pat your lap.
Establish a slow but insistent rhythm, imitating the pitter-patter of cat feet.

8 Reinforce the cuddling behavior.
When your cat settles in your lap, stroke her gently from the base of the neck, slowly down to the tip of the tail, and then back to the base of the neck. Say "good cat." Give her a treat.

Be Aware

- Cats purr at a frequency of approximately 26 to 45 hertz, approximately the same as an idling car engine. Replicate that frequency when trying to attract your cat.

- Cats are most attracted to their own scent. Place her favorite blanket in your lap. If you remain unable to get your cat to cuddle, repeat after dabbing a few drops of cat urine on your neck and wrists as perfume.

SIGNS A CAT DOESN'T LIKE YOU

- Cat urinates on you.

- Cat urinates on your clothes/belongings.

- Cat defecates on you.

- Cat defecates on your clothes/belongings.

- Cat approaches with eyes very wide, pupils constricted.

- Cat approaches with ears flattened against head.

- Cat scratches you.

- Cat spits at you.

- Cat snarls/hisses at you.

- Cat meows at you with an agitated, guttural tone.

- Cat bites you.

- Cat ignores you.

HOW TO CALM A
FRAZZLED CAT

1 Secure the perimeter.
Close the doors of the room or roll up the
car windows if traveling. Being agitated
can initiate a flight reflex in your cat.

2 Get down on the cat's level.
Approach the cat on your hands and
knees. Make very small, slow movements.
Do not show your teeth or narrow
your eyes.

3 Speak calmly and soothingly.
Tell your cat that everything is going to
be fine.

4 Massage your cat.
In a fluid gliding motion, rub along the
length of your cat's back from a spot
between his eyes all the way to the base

Play the harp.

81.   *Behavior*

of his tail. Return your hand to the spot between his eyes and repeat. Your cat will purr or relax his body when you stroke an area he responds to best; focus your massage in those areas. As you rub your cat, purr gently and tell him again that everything is going to be okay.

5   Play the harp.
Plucked string instruments trigger your cat's anti-stress hormones.

Be Aware
- Signs of a stressed cat include urinating outside the litter box, eating far more or far less than usual, sleeping far more or far less than usual, and bald patches from excessive grooming.
- Do not attempt to soothe your cat if you are feeling stressed yourself.

FELINE PREDICTORS

Natural Event	Indicator
Rain	Cat looks out window or washes her ears vigorously
Earthquake	Cat acts nervous, hides
Heavy Frost	Cat sits with back to the fire
Heavy Wind	Cat rushes about wildly, tearing at curtains

INSTANT SOLUTION

DISENTANGLE A KITTEN FROM A BALL OF YARN

Grasp the yarn ball in one hand; grasp the kitten by the scruff of the neck with the other. Extend your arms to pull the length of yarn away from the kitten. Grasp another piece of yarn closest to the kitten. Repeat.

HOW TO DEAL WITH A CAT WHO IS JEALOUS OF A NEW BABY

1. Rub baby lotion and baby powder on your skin.
Prior to the baby's arrival in the home, acclimate your cat to baby smells by wearing baby-scented products around the house.

2. Fill your house with the sound of a baby.
Purchase a recording of "baby sounds," such as crying, laughing, and gurgling, or begin making such sounds yourself. Play or make the sounds constantly while your cat is at home.

Show equal affection to your cat and the new baby alike.

3 Reward a positive response to the smells and noises.
When your cat reacts calmly to the crying baby sounds and smells, pet her and give her treats, or praise her.

4 Elevate your cat.
Before the new baby arrives, move the cat's sleeping place and litter box to a raised location. Cats feel most comfortable when they are high up and can monitor an unfamiliar situation.

5 Keep the baby away from the cat's playing areas, litter box, and feeding area. As the child ages, instruct him on how to properly treat a cat.

6 Show equal affection to your cat as you do to the new baby.

Be Aware

- Similar tactics apply to prepare a cat for the arrival of a new spouse or significant other; make your cat accustomed to the smells and sounds of the new person before he or she arrives, and allow the cat to first observe the new person from an elevated level.

- Cats frequently react to the arrival of baby toys and play equipment by spraying these items with urine or feces. Keep these items away from your cat until she has become comfortable with the baby.

- Pregnant women should not clean litter boxes, as litter boxes present some risk of toxoplasmosis, which can be fatal to unborn children.

INSTANT SOLUTION

CREATE A CAT FORT

Cut empty cardboard boxes to expose corrugation and stack with other boxes and carpet remnants to make a cat fort. Rub portions of the fort with catnip to increase interest.

INDEX

A
Abyssinian, 44–45
addiction, catnip, 46–49
aggressor cats, 26–28
allergies, cat, 61–65

B
baby, jealousy of, 85–88
bathing cat, 14
bed, getting cat out from under, 10–12
bites, 30
breeds
  hypoallergenic, 65
  personality traits, 44–45
British Shorthair, 44–45
burr removal, 50

C
calming frazzled cat, 80–82
carpeting, urine-stained, 18
cat bites, 30
cat fights, breaking up, 26–29
cat litter, 55, 88
catnip addiction, treating, 46–49
cleaning cat, 14
cuddling, encouraging, 75–78

D
dislike, signs of, 79
dog/cat comparisons, 66–67

E
exercise, 53–54

F
fear of mice, 70–73
fights, breaking up, 26–29
forts, cat, 89
frazzled cat, calming, 80–82
fur, removing burrs from, 50

H
hairball items, 74
hardwood, urine-stained, 19

home
  kitten-proofing,
    31–35
  toxic items found in,
    36–37
hypoallergenic
  breeds, 65

J jealousy of new baby,
    85–88

K kittens
  disentangling from
    yarn, 84
  making home safe
    for, 31–35
  weaning, 40–43
kitty litter, 55, 88

L litter, 55, 88
loneliness,
  preventing, 21

M Maine Coon, 44–45
mice, fear of, 70–73

N natural event predictions, feline, 83

new cat, introducing,
    22–25
Norwegian Forest Cat,
    44–45

O obesity, 51–54

P pee odor removal,
    15–20
  fresh odors, 15–17
  old odors, 17–20
Persian, 44–45
personality/breed
  mismatches, 44–45
play fighting, 28–29
predictions, feline, 83
purring, 78

R rescuing cat from tree,
    12–13

S safe space, creating for
    new cat, 22–24
Siamese, 44–45

T toilet training, 56–59
toxic household items,
    36–37

training
  activities, 60
  toilet, 56–59
trees, getting cat out
  of, 12–13

U upholstery, urine-
  stained, 19
urine odor removal,
  15–20
  fresh odors, 15–17
  old odors, 17–20

W washing cat, 14
weaning kitten, 40–43
weather/event
  predictions, feline, 83
weight issues, 51–54

Y yarn, disentangling
  kitten from, 84

ACKNOWLEDGMENTS

David Borgenicht would like to thank Sarah O'Brien, Steve Mockus, Jenny Kraemer, Brenda Brown, and Ben Winters for making this book happen. You're the cat's meow.

Ben H. Winters would like to thank Ingrid Johnson of Paws, Whispers and Claws, the Feline Hospital; the professionals and amateur enthusiasts alike at Catpert.com; and most of all, to Ann Simon and the many cats she has loved over the years.

ABOUT THE AUTHORS

David Borgenicht is the creator and coauthor of all the books in the *Worst-Case Scenario* series, and is president and publisher of Quirk Books (www.irreference.com). He is allergic to cats, but is nevertheless putty in their paws. He lives in Philadelphia.

Ben H. Winters is a writer living in Brooklyn, New York, where he doesn't have a cat at present, but will probably be getting one as soon as his kids are old enough to ask. Please check out Ben's other books in the *Worst-Case Scenario* series, and visit him at www.BenHWinters.com.

Brenda Brown is an illustrator and cartoonist whose work has been published in many books and publications, including the *Worst-Case Scenario* series, *Esquire*, *Reader's Digest*, *USA Weekend*, *21st Century Science & Technology*, the *Saturday Evening Post*, and the *National Enquirer*. Her Web site is www.webtoon.com.

MORE WORST-CASE SCENARIO PRODUCTS

VISIT THESE WEBSITES FOR MORE WORST-CASE SCENARIO PRODUCTS:

- ✪ Board games
  www.universitygames.com
- ✪ Gadgets
  www.protocoldesign.com
- ✪ Mobile
  www.namcogames.com
- ✪ Posters and puzzles
  www.aquariusimages.com/wcs.html

For updates, new scenarios, and more, visit:
www.worstcasescenarios.com

To order books visit:
www.chroniclebooks.com/worstcase

MORE WORST-CASE SCENARIOS

HANDBOOKS

- The Worst-Case Scenario Survival Handbook
- Travel
- Dating & Sex
- Golf
- Holidays
- Work
- College
- Weddings
- Parenting
- Extreme Edition
- Life

ALMANACS

- History
- Great Outdoors
- Politics

CALENDARS

- Daily Survival Calendar
- Daily Survival Calendar: Golf

POCKET GUIDES

- Dogs
- Breakups
- Retirement
- New York City
- Cats
- Meetings
- San Francisco
- Cars